NAVIGATING LIFE: WIND IN THE SAIL

LEARN ABOUT THE HOLY SPIRIT AND HIS MINISTRY OF LIFE

BRANDON PEK

Unless otherwise indicated, all Scripture quotations are taken from the *New King James Version of the Bible.*

Navigating Life: Wind in the Sail

ISBN: 978-981-18-0879-1

First edition, first print: May 2021

Contents

Soli Deo Gloria

INTRODUCTION

"Holy, Holy, Holy" in Isaiah 6:3 and Revelation 4:8 proclaims the Thrice Holy God we have in our Eternal Father, Jesus His Son and the Holy Spirit.

The Third Person of the Godhead was first introduced in the Book of Genesis. The awesome work of creation was brought forth by the Will of God, the Spoken Word and the Work of the Holy Spirit.

> *"In the beginning God created the heavens and the earth. Now the earth was formless and empty, darkness was over the surface of the deep, and the Spirit of God was hovering over the waters" (Genesis 1:1-2)*

In the Gospel according of Luke, the conception of the Christ was first announced to Mary. The miraculous virgin birth was brought forth by the Will of God, the Word incarnated by the power of the Holy Spirit.

> *"The Holy Spirit will come upon you, and the power of the Highest will overshadow you; therefore, also, that Holy One who is to be born will be called the Son of God." (Luke 1:35)*

After the Water Baptism of Jesus, the Holy Spirit descended upon Him. And by the Will of God the Father, His Beloved Son received the anointing of the Holy Spirit in full measure and His Ministry on earth was set to begin.

> *"When He had been baptized, Jesus came up immediately from the water; and behold, the heavens were opened to Him, and He saw the Spirit of God descending like a dove and alighting upon Him." (Matthew 3:16)*

The night before He went to the Cross, Jesus Himself spoke of the Holy Spirit to be given to believers. On the third day, by His own authority from His Father, He rose from the dead by the mighty power of the Holy Spirit.

> *"But if the Spirit of Him who raised Jesus from the dead dwells in you, He who raised Christ from the dead will also give life to your mortal bodies through His Spirit who dwells in you." (Romans 8:11)*

God the Father gave the glorified Jesus the Holy Spirit whom He sent to live in every believer with the mission to search and prepare the Bride for the everlasting union with Christ Himself.

> *"And the Spirit and the bride say, "Come!" And let him who hears say, "Come!" And let him who thirsts come. Whoever desires, let him take the water of life freely." (Revelation 22:17)*

This book seeks to illuminate the Third Person of the Holy Trinity in our lives and the Great Commission we now have in partnership with Him to testify and bear witness of Jesus in His Ministry of Life.

Blessings,
Brandon Pek

1. OF TYPES AND SHADOWS

"The wind blows where it wishes, and you hear the sound of it, but cannot tell where it comes from and where it goes. So is everyone who is born of the Spirit." (John 3:8)

Let's start with types and shadows in the Bible that help us begin to know the Person of the Holy Spirit. Ask for the Spirit of wisdom and revelation to enlighten our inner being, with eyes to see, ears to hear, and the heart of understanding (Ephesians 1:18, Matthew 13:16-17).

Types and Symbols

Here are some of the more familiar types and symbols we find in the Bible that are associated with the Holy Spirit:

- Wind – the invisible powerful work of the Holy Spirit.
- Fire – the Holiness of God and judgement of sin.
- Water – the refreshing, cleansing and washing of sins.
- Oil – the anointing for healing and God's works.
- Dove – the gentleness and peace of the Holy Spirit.

Jesus also described the Holy Spirit as "a fountain of water springing up into everlasting life" (John 4:14) and "rivers of living water" (John 7:38).

The Bible also uses "shadows" to show us the Person of the Holy Spirit in the Trinity and His Ministry in the New Covenant, two of these are found in the Book of Genesis.

Shadow I – Sacrifice of the Son

Abraham was asked to take his son, his only son Isaac, whom he loved, and offer him as a sacrifice on one of the mountains in the land of Moriah. Arriving on the third day, he told the two servants with him to stay put and await his return with his son (Genesis 22:2-5).

He took the wood and laid it on Isaac's back, and then taking the fire in his hand and a knife, the two set off on the climb. But, at the top of the mountain, God stopped him from the full act and provided a ram caught in a thicket by its horns in place of Isaac (Genesis 22:6-19).

When we read this, the quick association is to the Cross of Jesus. However, additionally in the background, we see the shadow of the posture and the role of the Holy Spirit in the ultimate Sacrifice that was to come:

- Isaac rode the donkey to the mountain for the sacrifice he was spared from. Our Lord Jesus rode one on Palms Sunday in the days leading to His Crucifixion.

- Isaac was spared but when the time came, God sent His only Son Jesus, not sparing Him on the Cross in fulfilment of the covenant promise of the Messiah.

- The two servants were told to wait in Isaac's case. At Calvary, the Holy Spirit and the angelic hosts stood down, restraining themselves from using their powers.

- The two servants received Abraham and Isaac back safely from the mountain top but the Holy Spirit had to endure the judgement of the Innocent Christ before raising Jesus from the dead on the third day.

In this story, Abraham and Isaac returned to the two servants and they went to Beersheba (Genesis 22:19) which means "Well of Seven", signifying divine completion and perfection, or also known as "Well of the Oath" where Abraham made peace with Abimelech for his legal right to the land that God promised him.

The redemption work of Jesus was complete and perfect, fulfilling the Oath that God swore by Himself. As Abraham dwelt at Beersheba, so we as spiritual descendants of the promise shall also abide in peace, resting in the perfect finished work of Christ Jesus through the Holy Spirit (Ephesians 1:7-14).

Shadow II: Bride of the Son

Later in Abraham's life when he was well advanced in age and blessed in all things by God, he instructed his eldest servant of his house that ruled over all that he had to go find Isaac a wife from his kindred. The servant obeyed and took with him ten of Abraham's camels with all the goods in his authority (Genesis 24:1-4, 10).

The servant came to a well in the city of Nahor in Mesopotamia, and found Rebekah who was a daughter of Abraham's kindred. When her family heard the servant's story, they consented. Rebekah herself was willing and received the gifts that the servant brought, and her house was also blessed with precious things (Genesis 24:10-58).

Likewise, after the Cross, the Holy Spirit was sent into the "City of Nahor" – meaning hot and dry place in "Mesopotamia" which is the world today – with the mission of looking for and preparing the "Bride (the

Church)" for Christ. He is empowered to give gifts to "the Bride", that is, whoever with the same faith as believing Abraham and who are willing (1 Corinthians 12:11).

God has blessed us believers with all spiritual blessings. The ten camels with the master's goods represent the gifts and blessings of the Holy Spirit to equip, prosper and prepare us as we await the coming of Jesus to receive His Bride (Ephesians 1:3, 3 John 2:2).

The bride for Isaac was found at the well drawing water. When the servant asked, Rebekah showed herself with a serving heart, tending to both the servant as well as the camels (Genesis 24:11-21). This is a picture of us at the well of salvation with hearts responding to the Holy Spirit.

Like Isaac's chosen bride Rebekah, we as believers who have demonstrated the same kind of faith as believing Abraham have become **kindreds of like spirit and faith who are blessed** with the patriarch, and are now God's chosen Bride (Galatians 3:9, John 15:16).

The Bible says that Isaac came from the way of Beer Lahai Roi which means "The Well of Him that lives and sees me". When out to meditate in the field one evening, Isaac received Rebekah. At the coming gathering in the clouds, the Holy Spirit will transport us to meet Jesus (Genesis 24:62-65, 1 Thessalonians 4:17).

Therefore, comfort one another that the Holy Spirit in us will bring those of us who are alive and remain to meet our Saviour and Lord in the air when the marriage supper of the lamb is due (Revelation 19:6-9).

2. TRIUNE MOVE OF GOD

"Therefore having been exalted to the right hand of God, and having received from the Father the promise of the Holy Spirit, He [Jesus] has poured forth this which you both see and hear." (Acts 2:33)

Jesus said that He will ask our Heavenly Father to send another comforter - the Holy Spirit. In the Greek, the word is "allos", meaning another of the very same kind. The Holy Spirit is fully God in the Trinity, and is described as having the same nature (John 14:15-18).

Trinity-At-Work

Our Heavenly Father, His Son Jesus and the Holy Spirit are One God. The Trinity is always in perfect harmony and has moved in unison throughout the history of mankind from Genesis to Revelation, and will also remain One through eternity.

In Genesis chapter 1, the Spirit of God was hovering over the waters of the earth that was formless and void. By the Sovereign Will of God, with the authority of the spoken Word and the power of the Holy Spirit working in unison, everything came into being.

In the same chapter at verse 26, the first direct reference of the Trinity in Creation was made when God said, "Let Us make man in Our image, according to Our likeness".

And in Genesis 2:7, the bible gives us an insight into the creation of man, "And the LORD God formed man of the dust of the ground, and breathed into his nostrils the breath of life; and man became a living soul." Man was the only creation that had that unique privilege of receiving the breath of life directly from God, became a living soul in a physical body.

The Trinity was also at work in the incarnation of Jesus. When the time was due, we learn that the Holy Spirit by the Will of God brought forth the miraculous virgin birth, bringing into the world the Messiah our Christ. The Word became flesh and dwelt among men as the only begotten Son of the Father (Luke 1:35, John 1:14).

After the baptism of Jesus, Heaven opened up and as He prayed, the Holy Spirit descended gloriously in visible form like a dove upon Him. Then, a voice came from Heaven which said, "You are my beloved Son; in You I am well pleased (Luke 3:21-22)."

In His ministry on earth, Jesus worked with the Holy Spirit to carry out the Father's Will, preaching and teaching, healing the sick, delivering the oppressed, and performing miracles. He led an exemplary prayer life in communion and fellowship with His Father and the Holy Spirit (Matthew 14:23, Luke 6:12, Mark 1:35).

In the redemption work at the Cross, we saw the posture and work of the Trinity. Jesus who knew no sin went to the Cross and took upon Himself the sins of the world. The wrath of God was poured out on His Son while the Holy Spirit stood down and waited for His time to raise Jesus from the dead (2 Corinthians 5:21).

Concerning His resurrection, Jesus declared His own authority from the Father to take up His life again after laying it down. After three days, in that authority the Father gave He rose again from the dead by the power of the Holy Spirit (John 10:18, Romans 8:11, Galatians 1:1).

Trinity in Our Walk

Throughout the Old and New Testaments, the Holy Spirit moved in power and might with various manifestations including the folding back of the Red Sea, unceasing supplies of oil and flour for the widow of Zarephath, healing and raising of the dead by Jesus, and the many acts of the Apostles.

The Holy Spirit now indwells those who believe and receive Jesus as Saviour and Lord. And His anointing will also come upon them to perform the continuing work of the Great Commission, with the promise that He will be with us always through the Holy Spirit, even to the end of the age (Matthew 28:18-20).

In our spiritual walk, the Trinity is also fully involved. In chapter 1 of the book of Ephesians, Paul the Apostle declared that we are the redeemed in Christ receiving all spiritual blessings from our Father, and we are sealed with the Holy Spirit of promise.

At the end of this age, the Father honours the Son as the King whose ministry is anointed by the Spirit. We see the Trinity in the first chapter of Genesis through the work of creation, and the final chapter of Revelation showed the throne of God and of the lamb with the Spirit and the bride, the glorious Church (Revelation 22).

Three-in-One Gift

How are we worthy to receive the promise of the Father, the Holy Spirit who will dwell with and in us forever, in the fullness of His Grace?

Simply put, we are not worthy. All have sinned and fall short of the Glory of God. But thanks be to God, Three-in-One, we are justified freely by His Grace through the redemption that is in Christ Jesus (Romans 3:23-26).

Consider that moment in time on the Cross when:

- Jesus, the Son of God hung on the "tree" so that those who believe can freely eat from this Tree of Life for redemption into eternity in Him the Christ.

- Father God watched His Son suffer a death He did not deserve so we will never be abandoned, and His wrath will never again be poured on us who are in Christ.

- Holy Spirit first stood down and when the time came, raised Jesus righteously so that we can now move in His power and might in our walk and ministry.

We are freely justified in His Blood to receive the promise of the Father. The Apostle Peter preached that when we repent and are baptized in the name of Jesus Christ for the remission of sins, we shall receive the gift of the Holy Spirit (Acts 2:38).

Be conscious of the finished work of Jesus that restored us into the communion and fellowship with God through the indwelling Holy Spirit and His role in our lives.

3. IN THE OLD TESTAMENT

"Create in me a clean heart, O God, and renew a steadfast spirit within me. Do not cast me away from Your presence, and do not take Your Holy Spirit from me." (Psalms 51:10-11)

"If anyone thirsts, let him come to Me and drink. He who believes in Me, as the Scripture has said, out of his heart will flow rivers of living water (John 7:37-39)." When Jesus said this, it was concerning the Holy Spirit who was then not yet given, because He was not yet glorified.

The Spirit Upon...

God breathed into the nostrils of Adam and he became a living being. This was described in Hebrew as breathing into man His "ruach" which means breath of life (Genesis 2:7). The Holy Spirit is the breath of God who gives life.

In the Garden, Adam was told that the day he ate of the tree of the knowledge of good and evil, he shall certainly surely die or in literal translation from Hebrew biblical text, "dying he shall die". When they disobeyed, the Holy Spirit left and spiritual death occurred though physical death was not immediate (Genesis 2:17).

Thereafter, the Holy Spirit no longer dwelt in man, that is, until the Day of Pentecost in the Book of Acts when man was restored in Christ - Praise be to God.

The Spirit of God certainly did not dwell in sinful flesh during the Old Testament times after the fall, and only came upon the Patriarchs and those He appointed such as Judges, Kings, Prophets and Priests. The anointing upon was divinely purposeful but not permanent. King David even expressed concern the Holy Spirit could be taken from him after he committed adultery (Psalms 51:11).

While the Holy Spirit came upon many appointed men in the Old Testament, He only remained continually with those whom He anointed for mighty deeds. Among them were Moses who led the great exodus out of Egypt, his successor Joshua who eventually entered the Promised Land, King David who established the united nation of Israel, and his son King Solomon who built the Temple.

It is interesting to read that there was one instance when the Spirit of God briefly came upon an unbeliever Balaam whom He influenced to give prophetic predictions and blessings upon God's covenant people (Numbers 24:1-4). This goes to show that the anointing was always for the Glory of God and to do His Will.

Sharing of The Anointing

By His special anointing, Moses was empowered to successfully lead the great exodus under the guidance of the Holy Spirit who was in the pillars of cloud by day and fire by night (Exodus 13:21).

When Moses complained to God about the great burden of leading and caring for the Israelites, He responded by anointing seventy chosen men to help Moses lead. God took a portion of the "anointing" on Moses and gave to these leaders to share in the huge responsibility over the three million Israelites (Numbers 11:16-17).

To build God's Tabernacle, Bezalel from the tribe of Judah was filled by the Spirit of God with wisdom, with understanding, with knowledge and with all kinds of skill. And He also appointed Aholiab to assist, and put wisdom into the hearts of all gifted artisan (Exodus 31:1-11).

The seventy leaders were anointed to help Moses lead and organize the great multitudes, and make many conquests and exploits with might and courage. The anointing of the Spirit was also upon Bezalel who was chief artisan for the building of the Tabernacle, and the same wisdom was shared by many other artisans to complete the tasks.

The Spirit of God moved among His people and anointed generations after generations of His covenant people. Joshua and the judges were anointed military leaders with judicial responsibilities over the nation and people of Israel (Deuteronomy 34:9, Judges 3:10, 6:31).

The anointing was also passed on to King Saul, and the special anointing on the successor King David and to the latter's son King Solomon, as well as the prophets and priests who served God in the court of these Kings (1 Samuel 10:6-10, 16:1-14, 1 Kings 4:29-34).

The Spirit of God came upon these Old Testament heroes and is the same Holy Spirit whom Jesus spoke about and the Apostles testified of, which believers have within and upon them today, giving various gifts to the body for the Ministry of Life (John 14:16-17, 14:25-26, 16:7-8, 16:13-15, Acts 1:5-8, 1 Corinthians 2:10-11, 12:7-11).

Covenant Witness and Enforcer

The Spirit of God was in the burning torch when the covenant was cut with Abram (Genesis 15:17-18), and He was also in the burning bush when Moses first encountered God (Exodus 3:2). He led the exodus in the pillars of cloud and fire, two elements typically used to describe the Holy Spirit (Exodus 13:21-22).

God also cut a covenant with King David, and the Holy Spirit worked to ensure that the covenant remained intact leading to the coming of the Messiah and the fulfilment of the main tenet of the Davidic covenant – "He shall build a house for my name, and I will establish the throne of his Kingdom for ever (2 Samuel 7:2-17)."

Both King David and his son King Solomon were anointed by the Holy Spirit but they could not completely fulfil their parts in the covenant (2 Samuel 12:7-14, 1 Kings 11:11-13). However, our covenant making and keeping God preserved the covenants even though His people could not fulfil their parts.

The Holy Spirit in the Old Testament was the Witness and Enforcer of the various covenants God cut with His people, enabling the coming of our Saviour and Lord Jesus through the line of David (Matthew 1:1).

When the time came, the Messiah our Christ fulfilled not only the Davidic covenant but all covenants that God had made by the power of God, the Holy Spirit. In the New Testament, He acts also on behalf of the Godhead as the seal and enforcer of the new and everlasting covenant.

4. SPIRIT TESTIFY OF JESUS

"And we are witnesses of these things; and so is the Holy Spirit, whom God has given to those who obey Him." (Acts 5:32)

Jesus promised the disciples that He will send another comforter of His same kind from the Heavenly Father. The Holy Spirit is our seal of the new covenant written in His Blood, the Spirit of promise who testify of Jesus our Christ and His perfect finished work (2 Corinthians 1:22).

The Holy Spirit in the New Testament

In the upper room, Jesus spoke of the role that the Holy Spirit has in the glorified ministry. He is:

- Comforter / Helper / Counsellor of the same kind as Jesus who dwells with and in us (John 14:15-18).
- Teacher of all things, reminding us what Jesus had taught and giving us peace (John 14:26-27).
- Spirit of Truth from the Father testifying of Jesus with those He had called and chosen (John 15:26-27).
- Guide into all truth, speaking on behalf of the Father and showing us things to come (John 16:13-15).

The Holy Spirit is the One who will convict the world of sin, and of righteousness, and of judgment. Unbelievers will be convicted of their sins, and those who are awakened and believe in Him will be imputed with His righteousness. And to the ruler of this world and his followers, they are already judged (John 16:8-11).

The Holy Spirit is the seal of the New Covenant in His Blood, unto the day of redemption (John 6:27, Ephesians 1:13, 4:30). He enables us to bear fruit, upon which He gives various spiritual gifts to equip us, support the work of the ministry and build up the church (Galatians 5:22-23, Romans 12:6-8, 1 Corinthians 12:8-10, 1 Peter 4:11).

When we walk by the Spirit, listening to and obeying His instructions, He works in and through us, empowering us individually and as His body for Kingdom work.

Bearing Witness of Christ

The Holy Spirit testifies of Jesus (John 15:26). In legal terms, the word "testify" refers to the act of providing evidence or proof that something exists or is the case. In other words, to bear witness. The person that testifies in court must be a credible witness.

The Holy Spirit, the Third Person of our Triune God, has the very same kind of Spirit as our Heavenly Father and His Son. He was with God before the foundation of the world and is God in and through all eternity within the Godhead. He is the credible Witness who testifies.

The disciples were also to testify of Jesus because they were with Him at the start of His ministry on earth but the Holy Spirit is the most credible of all witnesses because He is the Spirit of Truth who worked with Jesus from the time of creation to redemption, and continuing into the Ages to come.

The Holy Spirit can testify of everything in the Scriptures as He existed before creation with and as God. But there are vital testimonies that He will bear witness of concerning Jesus and His finished work.

The Holy Spirit testifies that Jesus is the One who came by water and blood; not with the water only, but with the water and with the blood (1 John 5:6). Water and blood symbolically pointed to the Word becoming flesh, that means Jesus came as God-man, or fully deity in the flesh.

The Holy Spirit testifies of the death and resurrection of Jesus as the Christ through whom we become partakers of the covenant written in His Blood so that we are fully forgiven of our sins and lawless acts (Hebrews 10:15-18). Jesus is the Lamb of God and there is no longer any other sacrifice for sin.

The Holy Spirit also testifies with our spirit that we are children of God when we receive the Spirit of adoption as sons and daughters by which we cry out, “Abba! Father!” (Romans 8:15-16). God is our Father and we are assured of sonship having the seal of the Holy Spirit of promise.

Three Witnesses to Key Truths

The Bible is inspired by the Holy Spirit, representing the Godhead, and is the testimony concerning the Father, His Son Jesus and Himself in God’s movement through creation, promise, redemption, restoration and revelation.

The Trinity is the Three that bear witness in Heaven and these Three are One (1 John 5:7). These testimonies of the Holy Spirit in the preceding sections establish that indeed in history, the present and the age to come that the following to be true:

- God the Father sent forth the Word who took on the human form and dwelt among men. We behold His Glory, the Glory as of the only begotten of the Father, full of Grace and Truth (John 1:14).

- The Word is Jesus who came as God-man, the only begotten Son, through virgin birth. He shall be called by His name Immanuel which translated means, "God with us" (Matthew 1:23).

- Jesus is the risen Christ and He has redeemed those that believe and accept Him who having been raised from the dead, is never to die again; death no longer is master over Him (Romans 6:9).

- The adoption of believers into the family of God as sons and daughters of the Lord God Almighty who declares that He will be a Father to us, and we shall be His children (2 Corinthians 6:18).

- Holy Spirit now dwells with and lives in believers forever as evidence of the above. Because we are God's children, the Spirit in our heart helps us cry out "Abba! Father!" (Galatians 4:6).

Our Triune God is the Witness Three-in-One who testifies of Jesus and our eternal position in Christ as sons and daughters of Lord God Almighty.

5. FRUIT OF OUR SPIRIT

"I will give you a new heart and put a new spirit within you; I will take the heart of stone out of your flesh and give you a heart of flesh.... And I will multiply the fruit of your trees and the increase of your fields, so that you need never again bear the reproach of famine among the nations." (Ezekiel 36:26-30)

The Holy Spirit is the spring within us that wells up to eternal life, nourishing with the Word of God in our inner man to bear fruits as good testimony. This is how we can testify of Jesus – not only by the refreshing spring but also by our fruit (John 4:14, Galatians 5:22).

Becoming Fruitful

Jesus told His disciples to abide in Him, and He in them, for He is the Vine and they are the branches. No branch on the tree can bear fruit by itself unless it remains in the vine (John 15:4-5).

Gentile believers who have been grafted into the olive tree now share with the natural branches the nourishing roots. There is neither Jew nor Gentile for we are all one in Christ Jesus. (Romans 11:17, Galatians 3:28).

Whether natural or grafted branches, that is Jewish or Gentile believers, we can only bear fruits as part of the Living Tree of Life drawing from the Holy Root.

As believers of the same Christ, God sees us all in the same light. We are branches sharing the same Holy Root of our Heavenly Father with Jesus the living Tree of Life, and the Holy Spirit providing nourishment for the branches to bear fruits.

The Word of God says that we will bear the fruit of the Spirit. There is only one fruit but with many parts, and of the very same kind because the tree is grown from one Seed – not of any seeds that are perishable but imperishable, that is, the living and enduring Word of God (1 Peter 1:23).

Christ died and was raised from the dead as the first born of those who are asleep (1 Corinthians 15:20). He was the Seed that had been sown by God, died and came back to life (1 Corinthians 15:35-38) so that the branches that grow on or are grafted into the Tree of His Resurrected Life can produce the fruit of His righteousness.

Fruit of the Spirit

Seeds sown to the flesh will from the flesh reap corruption, and there are many such as sexual immorality, impurity and debauchery, idolatry and witchcraft, hatred, discord, jealousy, fits of rage, selfish ambition, dissensions, factions and envy, drunkenness, orgies, etc…, leading to destruction, and they who do such things shall not inherit the Kingdom (Galatians 5:16-21, 6:7-8).

But, sow seeds of righteousness and we will reap mercy and eternal life (Hosea 10:12, Galatians 6:7-8) which is of the Spirit. When righteous seeds are sown, He will produce in our spirit the fruit of righteousness with the qualities of love, joy, peace, patience, kindness, goodness, faithfulness, gentleness, self-control (Galatians 5:22-23).

This fruit is the evidence that we are the children of God. Our spirit is first made alive in Christ (Ephesians 2:5), sustained by the Holy Spirit "the nourishing sap" that flows in and through us "the branches" extending from Jesus "the true Vine and Living Tree", drawing from our Heavenly Father "the Holy Roots." (Romans 11:17-18).

Fruitful Tree in His Garden

In one of his letters to the Thessalonian Church, Paul the Apostle exhorted the congregation to 'bear fruits as a body' (1 Thessalonians 5:8-22) through the following:

- Be watchful and sober, putting on the breastplate of faith and love, and as a helmet the hope of salvation. Also, Comfort each other and build up one another, just as they were already doing.

- Recognize and honour those who oversee and labour among them in love for their work's sake. Rejoice always, pray without ceasing, in everything give thanks; for this is the will of God in Christ Jesus.

- Warn those who are unruly, comfort the fainthearted, uphold the weak, be patient with all. See that no one seek revenge on anyone, but always pursue what is good both for themselves and for all.

- Do not let the fire of the Spirit be suppressed. Do not despise prophecies. Test all things; hold fast what is good. Abstain from every form of evil.

As branches on the same tree, while we are to be watchful and sober for ourselves, everyone ought to look out and help one another to be fruitful. Recognise and honour every member who labour in love, rejoice praying ceaselessly and give thanks.

We are to give caution, provide counsel and protect the weak, showing love and patience so that every branch will bear fruits in its season. Most critically, abide in the Word and be led by the Holy Spirit so we can test all things, holding fast to good and depart from evil.

Abide in His Word, walking in the Spirit that all of us will bear fruits in our season, giving individual or collective testimony of Jesus as Christ in our lives.

The Holy Spirit is given to guide us continually so we can be like a watered garden, and like a spring of water whose waters do not fail (Isaiah 58:11), where joy and gladness is found with thanksgiving and sound of singing.

Agree with and allow the flow of the Holy Spirit in our lives to deliver nourishment that produce the fruit, individually and collectively as a fruitful tree in the Garden, One united Church under Christ.

Our Heavenly Father desires to restore us, surpassing the glory of and fruitfulness in the Garden of Eden, for we have now a better covenant, which was established on better promises, Jesus our Christ (Hebrews 8:6).

6. THE SPIRIT REVEALS

"But also for this very reason, giving all diligence, add to your faith virtue, to virtue knowledge, to knowledge self-control, to self-control perseverance, to perseverance godliness, to godliness brotherly kindness, and to brotherly kindness love." (2 Peter 1:5-7)

Receiving the Holy Spirit is the critical step towards discerning the things of God which are revealed to us and freely given by His Spirit. No one knows these deep things except the Spirit of God (1 Corinthians 2:10-12).

The Deep Things of God

Described as "testimony of God", "Jesus Christ and Him crucified", and "the hidden wisdom of God ordained before the ages for our glory" (1 Corinthians 2:1-2, 7-8), these things are now revealed through His Spirit in the Gospel of Christ.

In order that we might know and understand them, we must first receive the Holy Spirit who will testify about Jesus as our Christ, teach us all things and reminds us what He had taught (John 14:26-27, 15:26).

In addition, the Holy Spirit will guide us into all truth. He will not speak on His own authority, but whatever He hears He will speak; and He will tell you things to come for God's Glory (John 16:13-15).

The Holy Spirit continues His mission to testify about Jesus Christ, and all that were said that He would do when the Spirit of God enters the hearts of believers and make His residence within. He will reveal the things of God and tell us things to come through the following:

- Spirit-inspired Scripture – on the road to Emmaus, Jesus explained to two disciples what was said in all the Scriptures concerning Himself (Luke 24:25-27).
- Fellowship in the Spirit – serve one another humbly in love, producing the fruit of righteousness, keeping in step with the Spirit (Galatians 5:13-14, 22-25).
- Diverse Spiritual gifts – by revelation, knowledge, prophesying, teaching, or in words made easy to understand (1 Corinthians 12:7-10, 14:6 and 9).
- Voice of the Spirit – Whatever He hears (from God) the Holy Spirit will speak and tell us things to come, guiding us into all truth (John 16:13-14).
- Praying in the Spirit – build ourselves up in the most holy faith and praying in the Holy Spirit, and pray also with understanding (Jude 1:20, 1 Corinthians 14:15).

Manifestation of the Spirit

The Holy Spirit uses the Scripture not only to teach and testify about Jesus but also to help us grow in spiritual maturity and be equipped for every good work prepared for us and rooted in Christ. All Scripture is by the inspiration of God and is profitable for doctrine, for reproof, for correction, for instruction or training in righteousness (2 Timothy 3:16).

As we grow in Grace and knowledge of Him, we will testify of Jesus by the fruit of our spirit and also through the manifestation of the Spirit that is dependent on our continued agreement and cooperation with the Holy Spirit. Have a willing heart and a yielded spirit. Abide in His Word, follow the teachings of Jesus and obey the leading of the Holy Spirit.

Build ourselves up. Be willing and ready for the Holy Spirit to operate His gifts through us. By His sovereign Will, God can raise the mountains and fold back the seas by the power of His might but He wants to work first in and through His children so that we shine as His lights in this world (Philippians 2:12-16).

It is the same Spirit who works all these things, giving to each of us as He wills for the benefit of all and the Glory of God. Be humble in spirit and learn from the Holy Spirit how we can manifest and operate effectively in His gifts, and discerning the spiritual as well as things to come (1 Corinthians 12:7-11):

- Revelation Gifts – word of wisdom, word of knowledge, discerning of spirits.
- Power Gifts – spirit of special faith, supernatural healings, working of miracles.
- Vocal Gifts – ability to prophesy, speak in different kinds of languages, and interpretation of tongues.

The revelations obtained from these spiritual gifts are to build up, encourage, and strengthen the Church. It is also a testimony of the Grace given according to the measure of Christ's gift, the salvation in His Blood (Ephesians 4:7).

Foundation System for Spiritual Impact

Having the indwelling of the Holy Spirt who helps us know and receive the things that have been freely given to us by God, including spiritual blessings and gifts. These are not understood and received through the senses but by revelation of the Spirit (1 Corinthians 2:12-16).

By His Grace, we can live and walk in love, peace and joy in the Holy Spirit, producing also patience, kindness and goodness, with exemplary faithfulness, gentleness and self-control in our words, conduct and actions (Galatians 5:22-25).

The fruit of our spirit is the baseline testimony that first satiates the thirst of pre-believers, upon which the spiritual gifts can manifest and operate with credibility when we bear witness of Jesus through the Holy Spirit to the Glory of God our Father in His Son (John 15:26-27).

There are also anointing or empowerment for those called into the five-fold ministry, and also supporting gifts to attend to the diversities of activities in different ministries from the same God who works all in all through His Spirit (1 Corinthians 12:4-6, 12:28-30, Ephesians 4:11-12).

Hear Him and listen to His voice, and be faithful partakers of Christ, encouraging one another daily. Be careful not to let unbelief turn you away from the living God in whom we find rest in Christ Jesus (Hebrews 3:12-15).

Pray in the Holy Spirit and also with understanding, building ourselves up on the most holy faith (Jude 1:20, 1 Corinthians 14:15).

7. EMPOWERING MINISTRY GIFTS

"And He Himself gave some to be apostles, some prophets, some evangelists, and some pastors and teachers, for the equipping of the saints for the work of ministry, for the edifying of the body of Christ." (Ephesians 4:11-12)

The manifestation of the Holy Spirit also empowers His chosen ones with special anointing to serve in different Ministries of high callings in the body of Christ.

Five-Fold Ministry

Among us, He will choose and appoint in these high callings for the equipping of the saints, for work of the ministry and building up of the body of Christ. No doubt that these ministers are themselves to be fruitful and exemplary in their walk for whoever are given much, from them much will be required as well (Luke 12:48).

- Apostles are way makers who forge new paths in the Kingdom and are a catalyst for change. They work in unreached corners in the world or places where the Christian faith is suppressed.
- Prophets accurately discern and reveal the heart of God for His people, helping them experience and learn to hear God's voice in their lives. They always lead His people back to the heart of God.

- Evangelists reach out to the lost and share the gospel. They partner strongly with the Holy Spirit to convict the world of sin, righteousness and judgement, with open invitation for all to join the Family of God.

- Pastors create a safe environment for believers to grow their faith, provide counsel to mend the broken hearted and heal wounded souls. They bring the local flock together as part of a greater global family.

- Teachers make the truth and knowledge about God accessible to all. They have the ability to break down the complex and clarify the Word, helping people know the Truth of God and apply it to their own lives.

We are familiar with the calling of evangelists, pastors and teachers, but some still argue the relevancy of the offices of apostles and prophets.

Paul the Apostle said that these ministries of apostles and prophets are to continue until "we all come to the unity of the faith and of the knowledge of the Son of God, to a perfect man, to the measure of the stature of the fullness of Christ (Ephesians 4:13-14)". We have not arrived.

Being Exemplary and Accountable

Serving in these Ministry gifts are typically full-time commitments confirmed by ordination with the laying on of the hands of the eldership (1 Timothy 4:14).

While ordination is not an absolute requirement for ministry, serving in these special ministry positions should require recognition and support from the local church and spiritual community.

Paul the Apostle laid the "qualifications" for bishop and elders in the church (1 Timothy 3:1-7, Titus 1:5-7). The same should therefore be applicable to ministers in these high callings. Here are the key attributes:

- Blameless as a steward of God, above reproach. Faithful husband to his wife.
- Manages his own house well, his children are faithful, not accused of rebellion to God.
- Temperate, sober, vigilant, sober-minded, prudent, and of good behaviour, orderly, respectable.
- Not given to wine, not violent, not greedy for money but given to hospitality.
- Holds fast the faithful word. Able, by sound doctrine, both to exhort and convict those who contradict.
- Not a novice or new convert lest being puffed up with pride he falls into the same condemnation as the devil.

These ministers need to be accountable, typically to the church, with demonstrated abilities or competencies to perform the duties required of them in their callings.

Whether bearing the fruit of the spirit, operating in the manifestation of His gifts in our walk or offices of high callings, we do so with the Holy Spirit's empowerment.

Glorified Ministry of Jesus

While each of the five-fold ministry has a very specific role in the body with different anointing flow from the Holy Spirit to perform them, there are key characteristics of the Ministry of Jesus on earth that we ought to learn from, both for our personal walk as well as ministry work:

- Heaven-centred Vision – fulfil the Will of God as Jesus did and not self-promoting (John 6:38).
- Holy Word-based – teach the Word of God and things pertaining to the Kingdom of Christ (Matthew 5:1-12).
- Holy Spirit dependent – perform the Work of God through the anointing within and upon (Luke 4:18).
- Heart and attitude of servanthood – meet the needs of others, not seeking service for ourselves (Mark 10:45).
- Honour in humility – serve God and the people, and He will exalt us in His Kingdom (Luke 22:26-30).
- Healing and deliverance – proclaim the Gospel, heal the sick and deliver the oppressed (Matthew 4:23).

Jesus made the sacrifice once for all and is now our High Priest forever according to the order of Melchizedek, King of Righteousness and Shalom Peace (Hebrews 7:14-17). We are called into the glorious body of our risen Christ, the chosen ones appointed into His royal priesthood ministry (1 Peter 2:9).

As priests of God and of Christ, we are also joint heirs in His Kingdom, having authority here on earth as His ambassadors to preach the gospel, the forgiveness of sins and the message of reconciliation (2 Corinthians 5:20-21).

The manifestation of the gifts of the Spirit empowers us in the glorified Ministry of Jesus, whether in our Christian walk, the five-fold ministry or supporting these.

8. SUPPORTING THE MINISTRY

"Every good gift and every perfect gift is from above, and comes down from the Father of lights, with whom there is no variation or shadow of turning." (James 1:17)

Do not marvel at the five-fold ministry with human admiration and think little of the many men and women supporting these ministries. We are one body with many parts supporting one another for the proper functioning of the whole (1 Corinthians 12:12-14).

Sharing the Honour

The body shares in the work of the ministry and thus also in any due recognition and honour, each receiving reward according to the work in His righteousness. With God there is no separation in the body. The Apostle Paul asked that believers care for one another especially those members who need special honour and greater care (1 Corinthians 12:22-27):

- Acknowledging the importance and necessity of those seemingly weaker members.
- Bestow greater honour on those members we see are in hidden or less honourable roles.
- Cover with greater modesty those members in less presentable tasks in the body.

The Holy Spirit gives different gifts to those who support the work of the ministry, according to the Grace given to them. Every part receives the anointing required for its proper functioning within the body (Romans 12:3-8).

There is diversity of gifts for the body. Some of these like ministry of Apostles, Prophets and Teachers have been addressed, while others are supporting gifts for the work of the ministry (1 Corinthians 12:28-30, Romans 12:6-8).

In the Book of Acts, we have the example of the Apostles appointing seven godly men to "serve at the tables" and support them so that the twelve could focus on the Word of God. As a result, the gospel of Christ spread and the disciples increased greatly (Acts 6:7).

Ministry workers supporting ministers or ministries are also important constituents of the Kingdom.

Examples of Supporting Gifts

The Holy Spirit gives different gifts but all working for the Glory of God and to do His Will. The following are examples of supporting gifts:

- Miracles – Corporate manifestation of gifts through word of wisdom, knowledge, faith in prophesy, healing and miracles, discerning of spirits, tongues and their interpretation.
- Leadership – Exhibits godly character, diligence and stewardship, full of the Holy Spirit and wisdom. Refers to leaders at all levels including elders and deacons, ministry and care group leaders.

- Serving and helps – Demonstrates love by meeting practical needs, usually through tangible work. Areas include car park wardens, security, ushering, logistics, multi-media services.

- Administration and Organizing – Perform routine functions, manages projects, organizing tasks or implementing them. This covers church office, ministry, outreach and other administration.

- Exhortation – Encourages believers to grow spiritually by discipling, teaching, and counselling them. Servers in various ministries, youth and care group involvement are anointed with such gifts.

- Giving – Conserves and shares resources, monetarily and otherwise, in order to meet needs. These could be through tithes and offerings, or giving to specific causes that the church supports.

- Mercy – Demonstrates God's love and compassion by responding to those who are hurting. Examples include grief counselling, hospital visitations, healing and intercessory prayer groups.

Serve with What We Have

Though man has sinned and fallen short of His Glory, the personality, natural talents and endowments continue to operate through the work of creation. These could be compassion, smart intellect, musical talents, hand skills, or other physical abilities.

We developed them as we grow, and may go on to acquire new or complimentary learned skills and abilities.

When these natural, acquired and learned endowments are used in the service of God, and with His anointing and spiritual giftings which only His children can receive, we are able to multiple the outcomes for God's Glory as we serve Him and one another as stewards of His varied Grace and gifts (John 6:1-14, 1 Peter 4:10-11).

So, by prayer and action, find our place in the body starting with what we already have or possess. Ask for His anointing and gifts as we look for opportunity to serve God in one or more of these ways:

- In our daily walk, as salt to the world and light that shines to the Glory of our Father (Matthew 5:13-16).
- In the market or workplace, performing heartily as to the Lord and not to men (Colossian 3:23)
- In local church or ministry, whether in leadership or supporting roles (Romans 12:3-8).
- In the mission fields, going into all the world and preaching the gospel to all creation (Mark 16:15).

There is no differentiation between fulltime, lay and volunteer workers for every member in the body are marked by their calling and service, and not by their employment status and titles.

Just as God had called and anointed those who are willing to give and build the Tabernacle in the wilderness (Exodus 35-39), He is calling us now to likewise build His Holy Temple and grow the Kingdom with whatever we have and the gifts we received (Mark 16:15-18, Luke 24:45-49, Matthew 28:18-20, 1 Peter 4:7-11).

9. LISTEN TO HIS VOICE

"Therefore, as the Holy Spirit says: "Today, if you will hear His voice, do not harden your hearts as in the rebellion,"" (Hebrews 3:7)

Fulfilling His promise of another Comforter, Jesus gave the Holy Spirit from our Heavenly Father on the Day of Pentecost. Many received the Holy Spirit as well as the Baptism of the Holy Spirit that day (Acts 2:1-12).

The Spirit of God is now in us and has a voice. He speaks what He hears from God and tells us what is to come (John 16:13).

God's Voice Out of the Scriptures

In the beginning, God spoke and created the heavens and the earth. Within the Godhead, and with Adam and his family, God had spoken and continued to do so throughout history according to Scriptures. For example:

- Book of Numbers – many instances when God spoke to Moses in personal instructional conversations.
- Psalm 29:3-4 & 68:33 – like "thunders and many waters", powerful and majestic, a mighty voice.
- 1 Kings 19:12 – after the strong wind, earthquake and fire, Elijah heard a gentle whisper or still small voice.

Hebrews 1:1 says that God in various ways spoke in time past to the fathers by the prophets, whether in loud commands, conversations or gentle whispers. And in the New Testament, God also spoke audibly:

- Matthew 3:16-17 & 17:5-6 – at the water baptism in river Jordan as well as transfiguration on Mt Hermon.
- Acts 9:3-4 – near Damascus, Saul the Pharisee heard a voice saying "Why do you persecute me"?
- Acts 10 & 18 – in separate occasions to Apostles Peter and Paul (formerly Saul) to teach and encourage them.

Throughout His Ministry on earth, Jesus spent lots of time talking with God. In what language? Well, in the spiritual language that perhaps only the Godhead understands.

Spiritual Utterance

The Holy Spirit will speak to us in His own voice. He does so from within and also speaks through us using our own language or enables us in another language which He did through the disciples in Acts chapter 2.

After the Holy Spirit was given on the Day of Pentecost, the first spirit-filled disciples spoke in other tongues and people who heard them were from all over the land. They were amazed the disciples spoke in their own languages. On that day, three thousand souls were saved. There were also many signs and wonders (Acts 2:1-12, 40-45).

It is the Holy Spirit who gives us utterance and He can help us interpret tongues even if they are spoken in unknown languages.

Regarding tongues, Paul the Apostle implored that when we speak in tongues, we pray also for the power to interpret so that the body understands, and unbelievers come to have faith in what they hear. Tongues without interpretation edify no one (1 Corinthians 14:4 & 13).

With the gift of tongues, ask God also to give us interpretation by the Holy Spirit. He may do so as you ask in prayer, or interpretation may come through the manifestation of His gifts (1 Corinthians 12:7-11).

- Word of wisdom for the divine guidance on the right application of knowledge, and what to say or do.
- Word of knowledge for the supernatural revelation of information and facts past, present or future not previously learned or acquired.
- Prophecy for the holy inspiration and prompting to proclaim the voice of God to the hearts of man

His Voice in Various Forms

In the Old Testament, God spoke through prophets and kings. Today, we are blessed with the Holy Scriptures (Old and New Testaments) to affirm the voice of the Holy Spirit who speaks through the Word and from within.

In His sovereign move, God may still speak from Heaven to large crowds (Matthew 3:17 & 17:5) or choose to speak to individuals in external audible voice as He did with Apostle Peter (Acts 10:9-16).

Mostly now, the Holy Spirit is that voice, our inner witness, that still small voice from the inside of us.

The difference from Elijah's experience is that this voice now comes from within us because the Holy Spirit now lives in us. It is likely in gentle intimate whispers that He speaks to us from within (John 16:13).

The Holy Spirit is the voice of God from within that will teach, lead and guide us, and intercede for us. He can speak to us through recognisable voice and language but also in other intangible ways:

- Affirmation, confirmation and illumination from reading and studying the Word of God.
- Peace and joy in the Holy Spirit according to the special faith from hearing and hearing His Word.
- Quickening in the spirit through inward prompting in our belly or rapid kindling of our spirit man.
- Open or inner visions, mental picture or image, a persisting word or statement, and confirmed by prayer.

The Holy Spirit also speaks through the manifestation of His gifts (discussed in previous chapters), and/or multitude of counsellors and wise ministers of the Word whom He anointed (Proverbs 11:14, 15:22, 24:6).

The Holy Spirit does not contradict His Word. Therefore, check in the Scriptures what we have heard, seen or read (Acts 17:11, 1 Thessalonians 5:21, 1 John 4:1-3), and having verified them, be doers of the spoken Word, and not just hearers for blessed are those who not only listen but also obey it (1 James 1:22, Luke 11:28).

10. PRAY IN THE HOLY SPIRIT

"Then there appeared to them divided tongues, as of fire, and one sat upon each of them. And they were all filled with the Holy Spirit and began to speak with other tongues, as the Spirit gave them utterance." (Acts 2:3-4)

Jesus led a prayerful life, waking up early to start the day praying in places where He could be alone with God. He prayed in all occasions and situations, preaching and teaching, and going about His Father's business. In the evening, He would do so and sometimes through the night (Matthew 14:23, Mark 6:46, Luke 6:12).

The Essential for Spiritual Life

Prayer is an important part of worship, seeking God in spirit and in truth, drawing near with confidence to His throne of Grace, receiving Mercy and finding Grace in time of need (John 4:24, Hebrew 4:16).

Prayer is communion and fellowship with God, walking with Him, joining together of our minds and spirits with the Father, His Son Jesus Christ and the Holy Spirit (1 John 1:3, 2 Corinthians 13:14).

Prayer is receiving impartation of the faith deposit in our spirit and obeying it. Be doers of His Word and share the gospel as ambassadors of Christ with full authority from the Kingdom of Heaven (James 1:22, 2 Corinthians 5:20).

Prayer is spiritual warfare. Take up and put on the full armour of God, pray always with all prayer and supplication in the Spirit, and be watchful as we wrestle not against flesh and blood. Persevere in prayer not only for ourselves but also over all saints (Ephesians 6:14-20).

Prayer is the Will of God in Christ Jesus for us as we do so without cease, rejoicing always and giving thanks in all circumstances because He hears and answers us (1 Thessalonians 5:16-18, 1 John 5:14-15).

Praying Varied Prayers

The following are the types of prayers mentioned in the New Testament that we likely do in combination:

- Imprecation (Matthew 5:44-45) – Pray in love and mercy for others as Sons and Daughters of God.
- Consecration (Matthew 26:39) – Pray to be set apart and be strengthened in Grace to do His Will.
- Faith (Mark 11:24) – Pray and believe that we have already received what we have asked for.
- Intercession (Romans 8:34) – Pray to intercede for others as He also intercedes for us and on our behalf.
- Agreement (1 Corinthians 1:10) – Pray in unity with the same mind and thought, and agreement in words.
- Supplication (Philippians 4:6) – Pray and present our requests with thanksgiving, receiving His peace.
- Worship (Hebrews 4:16) – Pray with confidence, drawing near to His throne of Grace.

- Thanksgiving (Hebrews 13:15) – Pray and offer Him praises and giving thanks to His name.
- Repentance (1 John 1:9) – Pray to receive forgiveness for our wrongs, and cleansing from unrighteousness.

Praying in the Spirit

Praying His Word is praying in the Spirit. When we do so, we are praying in line with the Holy Spirit, the breath of God who inspired all Scripture (2 Timothy 3:16).

- Jesus said to His disciples that "the words that He had spoken were spirit and life (John 6:63).
- The Apostle Paul taught that the Word of God is "the sword of the Spirit" (Ephesians 6:17).

With Word-based prayer, we speak life into our needs and situations, according to God's Will in His Word.

Praying in tongues, the gift of the Holy Spirit, is another form of praying in the Spirit. When we pray in tongues, there are noteworthy benefits:

- Communicating and communion with God, uttering mysteries by the Holy Spirit who searches and reveals the deep things of God (1 Corinthians 2:10-12, 14:2).
- Self-edification, receiving impartation from the Holy Spirit to build up oneself and promote spiritual growth (1 Corinthians 14:4).

With the gift of tongues, the spirit man prays but the whole being benefits – spirit, soul and body.

The third kind of praying in the Spirit is unusual. In our weakness, when we do not know what we should pray for as we ought, the Holy Spirit intercedes for us with such groanings which cannot be uttered (Romans 8:26-27).

- When Israel groaned in their slavery, God remembered His covenant with their forefathers and delivered them (Exodus 2:23-25).
- In the Gospel, Jesus groaned in the spirit twice before He raised Lazarus from the dead by the power of the Holy Spirit (John 11:33, 38-44).

With our groanings or cries for help, we have the Holy Spirit interceding for us and God will hear our cries.

Pray in the Holy Spirit and build up ourselves in the most holy faith to keep ourselves in the love of God, and maintain our focus on the mercy of Jesus that leads to eternal life (Jude 1:20-21).

Pray in the Holy Spirit and stir up whatever gift of God that He has given you. He has not given us a spirit of fear, but of power, of love and of sound mind so that we will triumph in our lives (2 Timothy 1:6-7).

Pray in the Holy Spirit and magnify God in our worship, giving thanks in adoration for who He is, and also continually offer the sacrifice of praise to Him for all that He has done and will do for us (Hebrews 13:15).

Pray in the Spirit – the Word of God, tongues and in wordless groanings – and all kinds of other prayers without cease for a spirit-enabled life.

11. SPIRIT ENABLED LIFE

"Now to Him who is able to do exceedingly abundantly above all that we ask or think, according to the power that works in us, to Him be glory in the church by Christ Jesus to all generations, forever and ever. Amen." (Ephesians 3:20-21)

Jesus said that He had come that we may have life, and have it more abundantly. He had since rendered us the Spirit of Promise who dwells with and in us, the seal of the covenant written in the Blood and enforcer of the latter on God's behalf (John 10:10, Hebrews 9:20, Ephesians 1:13).

Life More Abundantly

Spirit enabled life unlocks the abundance in the life that Jesus came to give. In the Greek, "abundance" simply means to have more than adequate supply. The following are some biblical references of this abundance that is beyond what we ask or think:

- Every vital and essential need in life will be added to those who seek first His Kingdom and righteousness (Matthew 6:33).
- Success and prosperity in everything that we do, and be in good health, even as it goes well with our souls (3 John 1:2).

- Grace abounding, always having all sufficiency in all things, and abundance for every good work (2 Corinthians 9:8).
- Joy and peace as we trust in him, so that we may overflow with hope by the power of the Holy Spirit (Romans 15:13).
- Eternal life as sons and daughters of God with every spiritual blessing in the heavenly places in Christ (Ephesians 1:3-6).

Jesus is the door to this life more abundantly and the Holy Spirit the key. Walk in His love, light and wisdom, redeeming and making best use of time to the Glory of God. Be filled with the Holy Spirit, praying always with all prayer and supplication in the Spirit (Ephesians 5:1-2, 8-10, 15-18, 6:18-20).

This does not mean losing control but simply yielding our flesh to the leading and guidance of the Holy Spirit. With His help, we are to take full and complete control over our flesh and worldly urges, and fill ourselves with His Spirit of life. Drink of Him and out of our hearts will flow rivers of living water that gush out and refresh those around us as well (John 7:37-38).

Living Kingdom Life

Crucify the flesh with its passions and desires, and pursue the Spirit enabled life in righteousness, peace and joy which is Kingdom life. The Bible is clear that those who do the works of the flesh will not inherit the Kingdom of God, but those who live and walk in the Spirit shall do so (Galatians 5:19-25, Romans 4:17, 1 Corinthians 6:9-11).

Chosen and called out of darkness into the Kingdom of His marvellous light, we now are His lights to the world. Therefore, walk as children of light. Abstain from sinful desires and do not use our freedom as an opportunity for the flesh but walk in His love which is of the Spirit (1 Peter 2:9-11, Ephesians 5:8, Galatians 5:13-15).

God loved us from the time of creation and this love has now seated us in Christ, in the bosom of our Father. Remain in this first love. Do not love the world or the things in the world. For all that is in the world – the lust of the flesh, the lust of the eyes, and the pride of life – is not of the Father but is of the world (1 John 2:15-17).

There will be trials and tests in this world but take heart in His peace that Jesus has overcome them (John 16:33). In Him, we have a High Priest who sympathize with our weaknesses as He was tempted in every way as we are, yet without sin (Hebrews 4:15).

Spirit enabled life is not of this world but the Kingdom of Heaven, the spiritual realm where Jesus reigns as King. It is walking in His light and love as new creation in Christ after the likeness of God in true righteousness and holiness with the help of the Spirit of Wisdom (Ephesians 4:22-24, 2 Corinthians 5:17).

Commissioned and Empowered

Spirit enabled life is a prayerful life that unlocks the abundance that Jesus came to give, with full authority of the Kingdom and power of the Holy Spirit for the Glory of God. It is fruitful and purposeful, empowering us for Kingdom work that we are commissioned to do.

Before His ascension, Jesus appeared to His disciples and gave the Great Commission which was recorded in the four Gospels, each pointing to the role of the Holy Spirit:

- Matthew 28:18-20 – Make disciples, baptising them in the name of the Father, Son and the Holy Spirit, teach them to observe His commandments.

- Mark 16:15-18 – Proclaim the gospel and baptise believers, with signs by the Holy Spirit following those who believe.

- Luke 24:45-49 – Preach repentance and forgiveness in His name, wait for the Promise of the Father and be endued with power from on high.

- John 20:21-23 – Shalom and be sent as Jesus was sent, receive the Holy Spirit, and proclaim the message of forgiveness and reconciliation.

Jesus had asked His disciple to wait for the Promise of the Father, saying that they shall be baptised with the Holy Spirit and receive power to bear witness of Him. And when the Day of Pentecost had fully come, the outpouring of the Holy Spirit was fulfilled (Acts 1:4-8, and Acts 2).

In Christ, we have authority and by the power of the Holy Spirit, we are to carry out His Great Commission to proclaim the gospel, preaching the message of repentance and forgiveness in His name, baptising those who believe, and teaching them His Commandments, that all may share in this eternal life, and have it more abundantly.

This is the Ministry of Life commissioned by Jesus, and enabled by the Holy Spirit.

12. THE MINISTRY OF LIFE

"..."Alleluia! For the Lord God Omnipotent reigns! Let us be glad and rejoice and give Him glory, for the marriage of the Lamb has come, and His wife has made herself ready."..." (Revelation 19:6-7)

"It is finished!" With these words, Jesus completed His work on the Cross (John 19:28-30). After three days, He was raised in glory and is now seated on the Father's right hand. He gave the Holy Spirit on the Day of Pentecost, thus beginning the Kingdom work and the Great Commission (Acts 2:1-4).

The Risen Christ

As public as His death was, Jesus was also seen in the open after He was raised from the dead, appearing to His disciples and many others for forty days. The Book of Acts began with a brief recount of what Jesus did through the Holy Spirit before His ascension (Acts 1:1-3):

- Performed miracles and teach as He did before the Cross (former accounts).
- Gave His commandments to the apostles whom He had chosen and appointed.
- Presented Himself alive after His suffering by many infallible proofs.

Jesus was seen by over five hundred brethren (1 Corinthians 15:6) during the forty days, teaching things pertaining to the Kingdom of God, spoken of in the Gospels but now firmly established by His death and resurrection.

It is noteworthy that He who had risen in glory with full authority from the Heavenly Father still did these things through the Holy Spirit. He had shown by example how His ministry is to be carried out as He commanded His disciples to wait in Jerusalem for the outpouring of the Holy Spirit (Acts 1:4-5).

This Great Commission, that we now share, came with forty days of living proof and eye witness accounts of His death and resurrection, His commandments, miracles and teachings pertaining to the Kingdom of God. Most importantly, He will be with us through the Promise of the Father, the Holy Spirit (Matthew 28:18-20, Acts 1:8).

Seal of His Victory

The Holy Spirit came as promised on the Day of Pentecost, and ever since, He has come to dwell with and live in all believers forever, with the anointing and empowerment as He wills for this Ministry of Life in this age (1 Corinthians 12:11).

The Holy Spirit has sealed us in Christ as children of God, co-heirs to the Kingdom, seated in Him far above all principality and power and might and dominion, and every name that is named, not only in this age but also in that which is to come (Ephesians 1:19-21, 1 Peter 3:22).

Our victory is complete and sealed by the Holy Spirit in His finished work on the Cross with assurance that:

- God loves us eternally. Nothing can separate us from His love revealed in Christ Jesus (Romans 8:38-39).
- God has blessed us with all spiritual blessings in the Heavenly places in Christ (Ephesians 1:3).
- God has forgiven and redeemed us through the Blood of His Son (Ephesians 1:7).
- God is faithful and He will establish us and guard us from the evil one (2 Thessalonians 3:3).
- God will raise us up with Jesus and we will receive our transformed bodies (1 Corinthians 15:42-53)

We have authority in His Name and power by the Holy Spirit to enforce this victory. The assurance from God's Grace and love through the Holy Spirit is peace and joy, so that in the face of tribulations, we can rejoice in the hope of the Glory of God (Romans 5:1-5).

Living Ministry of the Holy Spirit

When Jesus saw the multitudes, He was moved with compassion. He asked His disciples to pray for more labourers to be sent for "the plentiful harvest" (Matthew 9:35-38). The Holy Spirit with the same compassion wants us to work with Him answering the call to be sent.

In this plentiful harvest, there are those who plough the land, sow the seeds and weed out the ground in the days of former and latter rains. And there are those that reap, thresh and winnow. Yet others are in the storage and preservation work of the grain. Those who sow will rejoice with those who labour to reap this great harvest through the ministry and the church (John 4:35-38).

The Lord of the harvest are sending us as His mouthpiece and living testimony, co-labourers in the field through all seasons. We are in God's service working with the Holy Spirt who brings in the whitened harvest as we carry out the work in the fields (1 Corinthians 3:5-9).

As we labour in His love:

- Demonstrate this love for one another and to those who have yet to know the gospel (John 13:34-35).
- Persevere and not grow weary of doing good, for in due season we will reap (Galatians 6:9).
- Exercise Kingdom authority as His chosen ones, declaring His praises and mercy (1 Peter 2:9).
- Represent Him well as ambassadors for reconciliation of man to God through Christ (2 Corinthians 5:20).

Let us partner with the Holy Spirit in His Living Ministry for the Great Commission, and bring to the well of salvation as many as would believe and receive Christ as Saviour and Lord, and to minister and support one another in growth, preparing ourselves as the marriage supper of the lamb approaches.

13. FLOW, HOLY SPIRT

"...Grace to you and peace from Him who is and who was and who is to come, and from the seven Spirits who are before His throne..." (Revelations 1:4)

Before He went to the Cross, Jesus introduced to His disciples the Holy Spirit as another comforter from the Father. We know that the root word used in the Greek meant another of the same kind. He is not a force or energy, or magic that anyone can possess, but the Third Person in the Holy Trinity.

Names of the Holy Spirit

In Genesis 1:1-2, He was first mentioned as the Spirit of God hovering over the face of the waters. This is perhaps the common reference of His name in related forms:

- Spirit of God (Genesis 1:2, Matthew 3:16)
- Spirit of our God (1 Corinthians 6:11)
- Spirit of the Lord God (Isaiah 61:1)
- Spirit of the Lord (Luke 4:18, Judges 3:10)

In Genesis 2:7, He is also known as the breath of life when God formed Adam from dust, breathed into it and he became a living soul.

The word "breath" in Hebrew is the word "ruach" which is translated as the Spirit. From this Root name, He is also named in the Hebrew as "Ruach Elohim" Spirit of God, "Ruach YHWH" the Spirit of Yahweh, and "Ruach Hakodesh" literally the Holy Spirit.

In Isaiah 11:2, the Holy Spirit was also known as – The Spirit of the Lord, Wisdom and Understanding, Counsel and Might, Knowledge and as well as Spirit of the Fear of the Lord. And in Isaiah 11:4-5, He is as known as Spirit of Righteousness and Faithfulness.

In the New Testament, the Holy Spirit was introduced to His disciples in John 14:16-17 as Comforter, Counsellor, Helper and the Spirit of Truth. Other references include:

- Spirit of Glory (1 Peter 4:14)
- Spirit of Jesus (Acts 16:7, Philippians 1:19)
- Spirit of His Son (Galatians 4:6)
- Spirit of the Living God (2 Corinthians 3:3)
- Spirit of Holiness (Romans 1:4)
- Spirit of Grace (Hebrews 10:29)
- Spirit of Adoption (Romans 8:15)
- Spirit of Faith (2 Corinthians 4:13)

The Holy Spirit is as much a loving God as our Heavenly Father and His Son Jesus. He can be grieved and experiences joy. He is the Spirit of life who dwells with and in us. He speaks to us and gives spiritual gifts as He desires. The Holy Spirit is God.

Spirit Upon and Spirit Within

Gideon successfully led a small elite force against stronger foes. Samson was given superhuman strength to fight his enemies. The Holy Spirit came upon military leaders appointed as judges over Israel to empower them for service (Hebrews 11:32-35).

When Israel asked for a King over them, Prophet Samuel anointed Saul as their first King, and later King David as the successor (1 Samuel 9-10, 16:12-13). King Solomon was anointed by Priest Zadok (1 Kings 1:38-48).

Entering into the monarchic era of Israel, Prophets such as Samuel, Elijah, Isaiah and others were empowered by the Spirit of the Lord. Apostle Peter taught that prophecy never came by the will of man, but by prophets who spoke as they were moved by the Holy Spirit (2 Peter 1:20-21).

Judges, Prophets, Priests and Kings did not have the indwelling of the Holy Spirit but they were empowered for their appointed roles when the Spirit of the Lord came upon them. In some instance such as Samson and Saul, the anointing was lifted off when they turned away from Him (Judges 16:19-20, 1 Samuel 15:22-23, 26).

In His ministry on earth, being in the form of God and found in the appearance of man, Jesus humbled Himself and depended on the Holy Spirit to complete the work He was sent into the world for (Luke 4:18-19).

At the water baptism, the Holy Spirit descended upon Jesus who was fully God Himself (Luke 3:21-22). The Spirit then led Him to the wilderness where He was tested and triumphed. After that, He pronounced back in the synagogue that the Spirit of the Lord was upon Him, thus the beginning of His Ministry on earth (Luke 4:18).

Jesus worked with the Holy Spirit healing the sick, delivering the oppressed and performing miracles with signs and wonders, even in His resurrected form before His ascension. He asked the disciples to stay in the city until "they were clothed with power" indicating the Spirit coming upon them (Acts 1:1-3, 1:4-8, Luke 24:49).

The first infilling occurred on the Day of Pentecost and with the Spirit coming also upon them, the Apostles and other disciples performed various miracles and acts throughout their ministry (Read also Acts of the Apostles).

Today, the indwelling Spirit also comes upon us just as He did the Kings and holy men of the Old Testament.

Anointing for the Living Ministry

Now, every believer receives the Holy Spirit in them, the anointing within to help us bear the fruit of the spirit and operate in the gifts of the Holy One (1 Corinthians 3:16, 1 John 2:27, Galatians 5:22-23, 1 Corinthians 12:7-11).

As the Holy Spirit wills, we can also receive the anointing upon to continue the Living Ministry of the Spirit with strong empowerment, in full authority of His Name for the Great Commission, and the work of the ministry.

May we be filled with all joy and peace as we trust in Him, so that we may flow and overflow with hope by the power of the Holy Spirit (Romans 15:13).

THE BOTTOMLINE

There is no salvation in any other name under Heaven given among men by which we must be saved.

We were once sinners but have been delivered from the power of darkness and conveyed into the Kingdom of Christ, in whom we have redemption through His Blood, the forgiveness of sins. (Acts 4:12, Colossians 1:13-14)

Pray that this read has been a blessing. For those who have yet to receive Jesus as Saviour and Lord, there is no better time than now and today.

Salvation Call

God has made it so simple: "Believe in the Lord Jesus Christ and you will be saved". While we can receive His Salvation and Redemption in just one step of faith, it cost God dearly.

> *"For God so loved the world that He gave His only begotten Son, that whoever believes in Him should not perish but have everlasting life."*
>
> *John 3:16*

God becomes our "Abba Father" when we believe. There is now no more condemnation for those who are in Christ. The old is gone and the new has come. We have forgiveness of sins, and are now a new creation in Him.

"For you did not receive the spirit of bondage again to fear, but you received the Spirit of adoption by whom we cry out, Abba, Father."

Romans 8:15

God did not send His Son to condemn the world, but to love, heal and forgive. And whoever believes in Him will be saved by Grace and through faith, which is the gift of God. Through Him, as many as will believe, He gives life and life more abundantly to the everlasting.

"He who did not spare His own Son, but delivered Him up for us all, how shall He not with Him also freely give us all things?"

Romans 8:32

God raised Jesus from the dead and seated Him at His right hand in the heavenly places, far above all principality and power and might and dominion, and every name that is named, not only in this age but also in that which is to come.

"It is Christ who died, and furthermore is also risen, who is even at the right hand of God, who also makes intercession for us."

Romans 8:34

God's salvation is near us, in our mouth and in our heart, that if we confess with our mouth the Lord Jesus and believe in our heart that God has raised Him from the dead, we will be saved.

Finally, as an act of faith in the love and sacrifice of Jesus Christ, let us pray:

Lord Jesus,

Thank You for dying on the Cross for my sins. You are the risen Christ and today, as I receive You as my Saviour and Lord, I am raised up with You and seated with God in You.

Thank You that through Your precious Blood, I have salvation and redemption, the forgiveness of sins. God is now my Heavenly Father and I am His beloved child in You. I trust and follow You.

Abba Father,

Thank You for sending Your Son Jesus Christ to die for my sins that through Him I can have eternal salvation and redemption. Every time I call on Your name, You are here for me.

Thank You for the gift and fellowship of the Holy Spirit that fills me with joy and peace, showing me Your ways, teaching me all truths and guiding me in my walk to Your own Glory.

Thank You Abba Father, in the name of Jesus, Amen.

Now, let us rest in Him to the eternal Glory of God our Heavenly Father.

ABOUT THE BOATMAN

The Boat played a large part in the life and ministry of Jesus. It was mentioned many times in the Gospels, from the calling of the disciples to the days before He ascended back to Heaven. Its first mention in the New Testament was when Jesus sat in the boat and taught the multitude the Word of God from it.

After He had stopped speaking, Jesus instructed and blessed the fishermen with a great number of fish, and then called them to follow Him and be fishers of men. He and the disciples took the boat to many places, performing miracles onboard, on the waters and at the locations where the Word of God was taught.

After He died and was raised again, the boat played a part to affirm the great calling when the disciples caught a multitude of large fish from it. Jesus commissioned them not only to lead men to Salvation in Christ, but also to grow them to the fullest spiritually in the Word of God.

The Boatman desires therefore to helm that vessel from which the Word of God is taught, bringing the spiritual nourishment to wherever the Word reaches, and prayerfully, that it will help the children of God in certain measure of spiritual growth and maturity.

THE AUTHOR

Brandon Pek wrote and edited for corporate magazines and newsletter in his former careers, and now dedicates his writing interest to serve our Saviour and Lord Jesus as His "Boatman".

He writes for The Boatman Christian Fellowship (TBCF) and hopes to encourage and inspire believers to follow the example of Jesus and serve God in the marketplace and workplace, fulfilling their purpose and call to ministry in everyday interactions with those assigned to them.

 (www.facebook.com/theboatmanchristianfellowship)

 (www.instagram.com/theboatmanchristianfellowship)

Also by Brandon Pek

The "Navigating Life" series:

- *Navigating Life: My Logbook*
  Looking Back at the Various Christ Touchpoints

- *Navigating Life: Prayer Beacons*
  Guidance from the Lord's Prayer and Other References

Cover Image (Acknowledgement):
Photo by cottonbro from Pexels

www.ingramcontent.com/pod-product-compliance
Ingram Content Group UK Ltd.
Pitfield, Milton Keynes, MK11 3LW, UK
UKHW022010190726
13853UKWH00004B/1857